A Poetic *Journey* Around the World

TINA MICHELLE HENRIOT

WestBow Press books may be ordered through booksellers or by contacting:

WestBow Press
A Division of Thomas Nelson & Zondervan
1663 Liberty Drive
Bloomington, IN 47403
www.westbowpress.com
844.714.3454

ISBN: 978-1-6642-1240-4 (sc)
ISBN: 978-1-6642-1241-1 (e)

Library of Congress Control Number: 2020922642

Print information available on the last page.

WestBow Press rev. date: 11/26/2020

DEDICATION

I dedicate this book to my hero and husband, Horace, our six cherished children, my BFF siblings, and my always supportive parents. You teach me daily about the depth of God's love: truly, the best gift in all the world over.

Psalm 90:1-2
   Lord, through all the generations
you have been our home!
Before the mountains were born,
   before you gave birth to the earth and the world,
   from beginning to end, you are God.

Table of Contents

ADVENTURE

In all the world over- earth, ocean, and sky,
North, south, east and west- from dawn until night,
Wonder and reverence call us to discover,
To seek out adventure: it's there to uncover.

There's science and history, ancient and new.
There's invention and progress; tradition that's true.
There's art in all forms, and numbers precise-
And language, and culture, and virtue and vice.
Animals, insects, flora and fauna-
Micros and macros and fossils and lava.
We learn about health and what nourishes trust,
We learn about humans: what's right or unjust.

We see a glimpse of the glory of God.
We see what's good, or broken, or odd.

We scratch our heads, and learn some more.
We stand in awe, and commit to explore.
May heart, mind and body- feel, think and touch.
May our soul see the Lord who has given so much.

He gave His One Son, so we would not die.
And the Son rose again! We are loved, you and I!
And with every step in this journey on earth-
We give Him our praise, and share of His worth!

For though the whole world holds beauty- it's true:
The thing He loves most: it's me, and it's you.
And loving each other, diverse and unique-
Is the door to adventure.
Our God holds the key.

ALGERIA

Like couscous at the souk
I nourish
I am Algerian

Travel to the center of an Algerian city and you will find a bustling, open-air market full of goods and products from local farmers and craft makers, otherwise known as a souk. Here your senses will be engaged in the sights, sounds and tastes of Algeria! Mint, coriander and bright fruits and vegetables fill baskets. Fishmongers, bakers and butchers display their products, while buyers barter and bargain over prices as they inspect woven rugs, jewelry, metalwork and other crafts. An age-old commercial activity, shopping at a souk is a true Algerian experience.

As the most basic food in the Algerian diet, you will surely find couscous in abundance at the souk. This steamed semolina wheat is popular among all social classes and people groups. Indeed, couscous can be eaten at any meal (including dessert), accompanied by a variety of flavors. Sweet or savory, couscous is the national dish of Algeria.

KENYA

Like steam rising from a cup of hot tea
I will warm your heart
I am Kenyan

Kenya has gained international acclaim for their top export: tea! Kenyan tea is prized for its high level of antioxidants. Due to its nutrient-rich volcanic soils and tropical climate, Kenyan tea also has a distinctly vibrant color. Most Kenyan tea is grown by small-scale farmers, who sell their tea through the Kenya Tea Development Authority.

Kenya's agriculture is remarkable, as is its wildlife. The African elephant is the world's largest land mammal, and because of its large stature, it has no natural predator. Even still, African elephants are a threatened species, though Kenyan law prohibits ivory trade and elephant hunting. The elephants are a necessity for biodiversity and agriculture in a number of ways, including their impact on dispersing seeds and creating waterholes for other species.

NIGERIA

Like a butterfly
I am boldly beautiful
I am Nigerian

Nigerians are known for their kindness to strangers and willingness to share with others in need. This strong sense of community is stabilized by their respect for elders and often experienced through lavish and generous feasts! Chili peppers are often used in their sauces and soups along with an array of other delicious spices and herbs, creating quite a colorful and festive party.

The forests which border Nigeria and Cameroon hold the largest known numbers of different butterfly species in the world! In addition, they are home to the largest numbers of forest-restricted birds and mammals in Africa! Can you imagine the beauty and diversity you would see if you visited these forests for a day?

SOUTH AFRICA

Like those who dare to round the Cape
I am adventurous
I am South African

South Africa lies at the southernmost part of Africa and has been an important point of navigational and trading reference for centuries. The earliest of European explorers learned that rounding the Cape of Good Hope set their ships traveling toward the east, where they desired trade. Undaunted explorers from the east also rounded Africa's Cape of Good Hope in search of a route to Europe or the ends of the earth. As either rounded the cape, they approached the meeting point of the Atlantic and Indian Oceans.

But humans aren't the only ones who have eagerly rounded South Africa in droves. Each year an unexplained phenomenon occurs on the east coast of South Africa: a migration of sardines that can be compared to the Great Migration of the wildebeest across the African savanna! This teeming mass of sardines is so deep, wide and long that it can even be seen by satellite! And they're not alone. Predators like the great white shark, whales, dolphins and tens of thousands of birds plunge and gorge upon these sardines, creating a true hunting extravaganza, and all within view of inquisitive snorkelers and scuba divers.

ZAMBIA AND ZIMBABWE

Like moonbows glowing over stirring waters
I rise above
I am Zambian
I am Zimbabwean

On the border of present-day Zimbabwe and Zambia you will find the largest waterfall on earth: *Mosi-oa-Tunya*, meaning Smoke that Thunders. But perhaps you know this waterfall as the name given in 1855 when the first known European gazed upon the falls and named them after his queen: Victoria Falls. Both names are honored by the World Heritage List.

Whatever you choose to call them, this massive waterfall truly thunders.

Victoria Falls not only holds the record for greatest falling curtain of water on earth. It is here in Zimbabwe and Zambia that a unique and stunningly beautiful natural phenomenon occurs during the full moon: a moonbow. Moonbows, or lunar rainbows, are rarely found in nature and are rainbows that occur at night. Just after evening twilight or before morning dawn, moonbows are most easily seen in the sprays of the Smoke that Thunders.

CHINA

Like the Great Wall's extending stretch
My influence is far reaching
I am Chinese

The rich history and present legacy of China is colossal. You may be surprised by the amount of influence and strength China holds. In fact, China's population outnumbers the United States three times over, and its language is by far the most spoken language on the planet! Yes, the English-speaking westerner is a minority on this earth!

One example of China's feats is the Great Wall of China. The Great Wall is a symbol of China, stretching over 4,500 miles! This elaborate project was built throughout the lifetime of several emperors in order to protect the Chinese from their enemies. Over 2,000 years old, the Great Wall of China is truly a world wonder of historical significance.

INDIA

Like the colors of curry at market
I encourage discovery
I am Indian

Indian spices were a catalyst of the Age of Discovery, as merchants throughout Europe and Asia sought trade routes and intermingled in order to attain India's valuable and delicious delight. Still today, Indian flavor influences world cuisine throughout the east and west. Authentic Indian curry dishes incorporate various combinations of spices, herbs and chilies. Just as no two tigers have the same stripes, there are many combinations of curry flavor and cooking methods!

The endangered Bengal tiger is India's national animal. Though the Bengal tiger is the most common tiger, they remain at risk in the wild. As the largest member of the cat family, tigers are nocturnal hunters with great stamina and strength. Though they hunt and live alone, cubs typically stay with their mother for 2-3 years before establishing their own territory.

INDONESIA

Like the Puncak Jaya
I am strong
I am Indonesian

The Puncak Jaya is the highest mountain between the Himalayas and the Andes and the highest island peak in the world! Its power and beauty are admired by Indonesians, tourists and scientists. In fact, scientists are now concerned with collecting ice core samples from Puncak Jaya to assist in understanding ecological and atmospheric change.

Indonesia also has more active volcanoes than any other country and some of the largest volcanoes on earth! These volcanoes cause both fear and awe as they bring majestic explosions and deathly consequences. Mount Tambora's eruption of 1815 was the largest in recorded history, causing "The Year Without a Summer" across the Northern Hemisphere.

SAUDI ARABIA

Like green in the desert
My resources are precious
I am Saudi Arabian

Saudi Arabia is the largest country on the Arabian Peninsula, and over half of this land is covered in desert, including the Empty Quarter. The Empty Quarter is one of the world's largest deserts, some of which has never been explored! In the north of Saudi Arabia is the Great Nafud desert, known for its violent sandstorms and immense dunes. Running through Saudi Arabia is the Ad Dahna, a narrow desert which links the Empty Quarter and the Great Nafud.

But sand isn't the only thing found in Saudi Arabia! Two prominent riches lie within the earth of this land: oil and water. As the world's top exporter of oil, Saudi Arabia is famous for its oil supply. However, NASA satellites have images that suggest something more precious than oil is being drilled in Saudi Arabia: water! In the middle of the desert, wheat and other crops are growing due to the discovery of underground rivers and lakes full of fossil water. How long this non-renewable resource will last is a mystery. But in the meantime, green crops growing in the desert are priceless and precious!

TAIWAN

Like the contrast of Sun Moon Lake
I respect both progress and tradition
I am Taiwanese

In the city of Taipei, you will find what is currently the tallest and largest green building in the world! Though the skyscraper does have glass of blue-green hue, the term "green" is being used here to describe something that benefits and supports the environment. Taipei 101 was built in 2004 and represents both Asian traditions and modern progress. Indeed, Taiwan is known for its high-tech industry around the world.

Taiwan is not only known for its advanced technology and impressive cities. This leaf-shaped island is full of dense mountain ranges and serene lakes. The largest lake found in the middle of Taiwan is Sun Moon Lake. One side of this lake is shaped like the crescent moon, while the other is a diamond. Just as the sun and the moon represent two extreme phenomena, one finds modern sophistication and ancient simplicity in the country of Taiwan.

AUSTRALIA

AUSTRALIA

Like shifting hues of red in the setting sun
I am intricate
I am Australian

Uluru is the Aboriginal name for the monolith, or massive stone, found in what is referred to as Australia's Red Centre. Surface oxidation of the iron content in the arkose sandstone gives the Uluru a reddish-orange hue, creating exquisite displays of color, especially at sunrise and sunset. An icon of Australian folklore, this land of tantalizing reds was re-gifted back to the indigenous Aboriginal people from the Australian government in 1985, and is now jointly managed.

Long before Australia was colonized by Europeans, the indigenous Aboriginals held a meteorological view of seasonal change far more intricate and diverse than the western climate descriptions of spring, summer, fall and winter. Instead, Aboriginals find it pertinent to describe five to six seasons! Throughout Australia's immense ecological zones and regions, these cycles are described based on changing events in the natural world. Survival and success in vast Australia are dependent on this acute awareness of seasonal prediction, also referred to by present day meteorologists.

FRENCH POLYNESIA

Like a lustrous black pearl
I shimmer
I am French Polynesian

French Polynesia is a collection of islands surrounded by thick, flourishing reefs and shimmering clear-blue lagoons. Lagoons are shallow and quiet waters, undisturbed by rough ocean waves due to protective barriers such as islands or sandbars. Teeming with coral, dolphins, sea turtles and other marine life, French Polynesia is home to the second largest lagoon in the world: Rangiroa.

Within the Tuamotu lagoons lives an animal which gives French Polynesia their greatest export: the black pearl. The Tahitian black pearl is indigenous to the South Pacific and is produced only through the giant black-lipped oyster. Pearls are formed when an unwanted foreign object enters an oyster's mantle. Protecting itself, the oyster covers the irritant with layers of a mucus-like structure called nacre, and over time it creates a pearl. The under color of a giant black-lipped oyster's pearl ranges from pale silver to deep black, and may be layered in a rainbow of iridescent hues.

NEW ZEALAND

Like a Dark Sky Reserve exposing millions of stars
I reflect glory
I am a New Zealander

From the depths of the earth to the highest of heavens, New Zealand offers captivating wonders mirroring the grandeur of the universe. Deep within the Waitomo Caves of New Zealand's North Island, wander through dark paths, discovering its famous limestone shaft and acoustic cathedral cavern. Especially unique within the Waitomo Caves are the glowworms who live there, found nowhere else on planet earth! These tiny, twinkling creatures cling to the cave ceiling over the underground Waitomo River, creating the illusion of an underground galaxy.

Standing above ground on the South Island of New Zealand, you will find another magnificent, twinkling site in the Mackenzie Basin. With uncorrupted, pristine skies and nocturnal darkness that reveal a blanket of stars, this is designated as an international Dark Sky Reserve and one of the best stargazing sites on the planet. Gazing at millions of stars in the heavens will trigger wonder: this universe is full of glory!

SOLOMON ISLANDS

Like the building of a coral reef
I develop
I am a Solomon Islander

Perhaps you know that islands are made by the mounting lava of underwater volcanoes. Thus is the case for the Solomon Islands. The most southern of the Solomon Islands is named Rennell Island, and it is in East Rennell that two world wonders exist! After the lava cooled which created the island, tiny sea animals called coral began to build a reef in the surrounding water. These animals have a strong exoskeleton of limestone, and billions of

these exoskeletons are found in the reef! The East Rennell reef has a ring-shape, making it a coral atoll. East Rennell is where you find the largest raised coral atoll in the world!

Coral atolls surround bodies of water called lagoons. The former lagoon for East Rennell's coral atoll is Lake Tegano. This is the largest lake in the insular Pacific where many endemic species live. One of the native animals living in these waters is the sea krait, *Laticauda crockeri,* otherwise known as a sea snake! Found only here, this particular sea snake actually lives in fresh water, a rarity indeed!

TONGA

Like the full flavor of vanilla
I am friendly
I am Tongan

Tonga was given the name the Friendly Islands after Captain James Cook visited Tonga for the first time in 1773. He was invited to the *inasi* festival, where yams were donated to the island's head chief each year. It is speculated that the chiefs desired to kill him at this festival, but could not agree on a plan! In any case, Tonga is proud to be the only monarchy in the South Pacific that has never been colonized!

Yams and squash are still a main crop in Tonga, along with vanilla beans. Tongan plantations with rich and fertile soil create a splendid spot for the organic growing of vanilla vines. The vanilla beans produced are used by gourmet chocolate makers and astute chefs worldwide who search for bold, unique and full vanilla flavors.

BELGIUM

Like a box of gourmet Belgian truffles
I hold lots of important pieces
I am Belgian

Belgian chocolate is known around the world for its gourmet taste and quality. Today, many are also concerned that the ingredients used in this sweet indulgence come to them in a fair and humane manner. Belgian chocolatiers are known to use the finest cocoa beans in their delectable product. Perhaps you'd like to eat a piece of Belgian chocolate after you

finish your Belgian Brussel sprouts?

Political councils of international importance such as the European Parliament gather in Brussels, Belgium. The European Parliament is the elected body that represents the European Union. It exists to serve its citizens in both civil and political matters, often forming legislation and policies alongside the Council of Ministers who represent its Member States. Thus, Brussels unofficially calls itself the capital of Europe.

ESTONIA

Like elves among ancient trees
I harbor magical memories
I am Estonian

Like a real-life fairytale, Estonia is full of ancient forests and flourishing meadows. Forests cover over half of the country, and one third of these forests are protected. In fact, you can discover types of primeval forest cover in Estonia not found in other parts of Europe. Primeval forest cover is unique because humans have not tampered in this nature for centuries, allowing higher amounts of biodiversity to birth in the forest's ecosystem.

Unlike primeval forests, meadows are formed through human activities like mowing and grazing. The meadows of Estonia are chock-full of botanic life. The variety of color, flora and species found in the wooded meadows make them distinct in all of Europe. Rare northern orchids, endangered animals and grazing sheep all find their home in the meadows of Estonia.

GERMANY

Like words by Brothers Grimm on a printed page
I am clearly creative
I am German

If you think you're unfamiliar with Jacob and Wilhelm Grimm, guess again. At the turn of the 19th century these two brothers became intrigued with German folktales. Over time they modified and created some of the best known tales and legends of our day. Stories like Hansel and Gretel, Rapunzel, and Rumpelstiltskin were popularized by the Brothers Grimm.

However, the Brothers Grimm would never have had such wide publication if another German hadn't invented the printing press almost 400 years before they were born. In 1440 Johannes Gutenberg invented a machine that changed the world dramatically. In fact, many call the printing press the most important contribution to civilization in the last 1,000 years! Due to the printing press, ideas and stories could be exchanged at an unprecedented rate. Thanks to Johannes Gutenberg you can read this book today!

NORWAY

Like Vikings in days of old
I'm not afraid of the journey
I am Norwegian

Many Norwegians live within a few miles of the sea, and these deep waters have always played a major role in their history, culture and livelihood. The Vikings of Norway lived from the 8th to 11th centuries and were the first to cross the Atlantic Ocean. The voyages of Vikings like Erik the Red and his son, Lief Erikson, led to outstanding discoveries and infamous battles. But humans aren't the only ones who have taken perilous journeys in the waters of Norway.

From freshwater to open sea, Atlantic salmon are known for their long and dangerous journey that constantly puts them at mortal risk. Transferring nutrients across diverse waters, the salmon's lifelong journey plays an important ecological role. This iconic fish causes scientists to marvel at their stamina and fishermen to long for a bite. As the world's top producer of Atlantic salmon, Norway's economy is strongly supported by the export of salmon and other related commodities.

PORTUGAL

Like art upon earthen clay
I celebrate
I am Portuguese

Every day, wood burning kilns are busy heating authentic Portuguese pottery throughout Portugal. Known as "Pottery Heaven", Portugal's tiles and pottery are sought after worldwide. Each region has a specialized style and earthen color, but all are known for their quality and design. Due to Portugal's historic diversity, several cultures have influenced their decor and motifs. This makes Portuguese ceramics distinguishable and richly artistic.

Portugal is also known as the world's top cork producer. Hearing the *pop* of a cork being released from a bottle brings thoughts of celebration and joy. Indeed, the harvesting of cork itself is also cause for celebration! Cork is harvested from its outer bark, which is able to regenerate! Therefore, there is no need to cut down the tree when harvesting, protecting the support system of endemic plants and endangered animals.

BAHAMAS

Like the pink of a flamingo
I am lovely
I am Bahamian

The Bahamian national bird is the only bird in the world who feeds with its bill upside down! Consuming plenty of microscopic plants and animals, brine shrimp and other foods rich in beta-carotene, flamingos acquire their lovely pink hue. But West-Indian flamingos are not born pink. Covered with fluffy white down, they receive their pink tint with

time, after both mother and father feed the chick red milk, also rich in beta-carotene, from a gland in their neck.

The Bahamian national dish is conch, a white meat found within a rose-colored shell. Served in salads, hors d'oeuvres, chowders or main dishes, this popular food is cooked in a number of ways. Fried, steamed, marinated, stewed or scorched, conch is a beloved Bahamian delicacy, worthy of its status in this stunning country.

CANADA

Like the gravitational attraction between moon and earth
I make waves
I am Canadian

The highest tides in the world occur in Nova Scotia, Canada. What is a tide? Though an ancient phenomenon, the mysterious cause of tides was finally explained by Isaac Newton only three short centuries ago. Tides are the rise and fall of sea levels that occur due to the gravitational attraction between the moon and rotating planet earth. In the Bay of Fundy's Minas Basin, water levels rise an enormous 52 feet higher during high tide than low tide.

To put this in perspective, the volume of water flowing through the Minas Channel north of Blomidon twice a day is equal to the combined volume of every stream and river in the world! What power! These sloshing, churning waters create a roar heard throughout the area near mid-tide, making this turbulent phenomenon a seriously soul-quaking reality!

EL SALVADOR

Like an ancient community preserved
I awaken
I am El Salvadoran

What if you knew that in the future scientists would be studying your bedroom, your school and everything in them? The people of Joya de Cerén probably could not have imagined this either, yet their town has been astonishingly preserved under layers of volcanic ash for over 1,400 years, thus giving a clear look into a Mesoamerican farming community of the 6th century!

Apparently, an earthquake warned residents of Joya de Cerén to flee, as no human remains have been found in the community. Left behind were home, civic and religious buildings with amazing artifacts. Even perishable material such as beans in baskets and thatched roofs have remained intact! From cooking utensils to fruit trees, Joya de Cerén's ancient community awakens us to history and holds incredible value for scientists and archeologists.

GUATEMALA

Like Mayan ruins
I speak volumes
I am Guatemalan

Within Guatemala lies one of the only World Heritage sites accepted for both its natural and cultural criteria: Tikal National Park. This park not only holds the largest area of tropical rainforest in Central America, but also Mayan ruins of an ancient metropolis! As the largest excavated site on the continent, Tikal, translated Place of Voices, speaks to us about the powerful Mayan civilization which lived here from 600 BC to 900 AD.

Through these remains, archaeologists are able to study the past evolution of Mayan culture, from hunter-gathering to farming. Palaces, temples, water reservoirs and ball courts are just a few of the incredible ruins which highlight their economic, political and social organization. Truly, Tikal National Park speaks volumes about Guatemalan history!

UNITED STATES OF AMERICA

Like Lady Liberty's torch
I shine
I am American

What 225-ton gift from France came across the Atlantic Ocean in 350 pieces to celebrate our nation's centennial? The beautiful Statue of Liberty! The Statue of Liberty has become more than a copper monument in our country. She is a face of freedom and hope to the world. Seven rays shine from her crown, representing the seven continents, while the chains of oppression and tyranny lie broken at her feet. As she holds a torch of light high in her right hand, her left hand holds a tablet with the Roman numerals, "July 4th, 1776," the birth date of our nation.

However, thousands of years before the USA became a nation, indigenous Americans inhabited the land. Across the country, American Indian tribes of diverse languages and ways of life lived among forests, plateaus, deserts and cities of stone. Ancient artifacts tell stories of their beliefs, customs and interaction with nature. Be sure to search for arrowheads and other artifacts in your own backyard, for though our nation is young, its history is old.

ARGENTINA

Like a polo pony in a chukka
I am vivacious
I am Argentine

Argentine polo is considered the best in the world! Though polo is one of the oldest team sports on the planet, polo was not brought to Argentina until the late 1800's. Argentine gauchos were already playing pato on horseback, which also requires hand-eye coordination with a ball on the field. The game of pato made the adaptation to polo seamless, as polo is best described as hockey on a horse. Argentina now dominates this sport as world champions and is home to most of the world's top players!

But polo players aren't the only top athletes in Argentina! A large part of their polo success is due to their Argentine polo ponies. Though referred to as ponies in the sport of polo, these animals are actually horses of Thoroughbred and Criollo blood. Admired for their aptitude and speed on the polo field, Argentine polo ponies are desired by players worldwide. Case in point, the Argentine Open is the most important polo match in the world and utilizes over 64 polo ponies and only 8 human players over 8 periods, referred to as chukkas.

BOLIVIA

Like long lines of dino tracks
I tell a story
I am Bolivian

Bolivia has an intriguing history that draws us into stories of an ancient people renowned for their thriving civilization. The Tiahuanaco lived between AD 500-900 on the second largest lake in South America, Lake Titicaca. Establishing themselves as a religious, political and trading center before the Incas even existed, the Tiahuanaco built sophisticated road, irrigation and agricultural systems that provided a way to grow crops in unproductive soil. Tiahuanaco relics and remains from their impressive city can be found in Bolivian museums today.

But there are other artifacts in Bolivia which date even farther back in history! Over 5,000 dinosaur footprints exist on a large sedimentary rock face at Cal Orcko, near the capital of Bolivia. These dinosaur tracks are thought to consist of over 300 dinosaur species! In fact, the limestone slab covered in tracks is one of the most significant collections of dinosaur footprints in the world!

CHILE

Like teetering toward the end of the world
I hold you in suspense
I am Chilean

The skinny country of Chile stretches so far north and south that it has an abundant variety of wildlife and weather. In the north of Chile is the Atacama Desert, known as the world's driest desert. There are coastal plains, volcanoes, geysers and hot springs in the Atacama Desert, but very few living things can survive such extreme conditions. Even bacteria and insects are not found in some parts of the Atacama!

However, as you travel to the southernmost part of Chile, you will find the Tierra del Fuego, "Land of Fire", which isn't named for its heat! Indeed, Tierra del Fuego possesses polar or sub-Antarctic climates. Several species of penguins enjoy the glaciers and icy beaches alongside bundled adventurers looking to experience what early explorers once called the end of the earth as they rounded Cape Horn by ship. Trying to prove the earth wasn't flat, these explorers fortunately discovered they were correct!

ECUADOR

Like the lifespan of a Galapagos tortoise
I endure
I am Ecuadorian

Ecuadorians express admiration for their beautiful landscapes, towns and regions through pasillo, their national music genre. Pasillo music crosses all social boundaries, unifying Ecuadorians in pride for their country. As pasillo is associated with the South American Wars of Independence, it provokes feelings of Ecuadorian nationalism. Pasillo music has a melancholy melody and poetic lyrics, the perfect rhythm for an easy-going Galapagos tortoise!

The Galapagos tortoise gets up in the morning and basks in the sun. After a lackadaisical day of grazing on vegetation, it retires in the late afternoon to sleep in mud, water or dense brush. Though impressive in weight and length, its true wonder is found as the world's longest-lived of all vertebrates: over 100 years!

PERU

Like the Inca Empire
I am mysteriously marvelous
I am Peruvian

From the Peruvian Andes came a people who built a fascinating pre-Columbian civilization, the Incas. The Inca Empire lasted from at least the early 1400's to 1532. Their highly developed culture left evidence of mysterious technological and engineering advances. Wonders such as suspension bridges and a specialized language using knots leave us marveling at their innovation.

One of the Inca's most stunning legacies was their ability to build cities of stone without wheels, iron tools or draft animals! Their architectural feats were made possible by those in specialized professions and the sweat of laboring citizens fulfilling their annual tax service. Transporting massive blocks over difficult terrain required sophisticated organization and engineering skills, not to mention strength! Stonemasons would then carve and shape the stones so precisely that no mortar was required for them to fit together and stay! Ancient Inca ruins still stand after five centuries of weather and earthquakes in Peru.

Author Biography

Tina Henriot has a bachelor's degree from the Ohio State University in Human Ecology with a specialization in Early Childhood Development and Education, a Masters from Liberty Baptist Theological Seminary in Religion with a Specialization in Pastoral Counseling, and was a former teacher and Cambridge Primary Programme Coordinator for an International school in Brussels, Belgium. She lived in Leuven, Belgium and sat on the pastoral team of CityLife Leuven, where she learned to speak Flemish. Today, she and her husband own and operate Play Polo Club in Westerville, Ohio, where they reside with their six children, two dogs, a cat, and over 20 horses. She is the author of "*A Polo Pony Fable: Prince and Pampita*", and enjoys announcing polo matches on the weekends.

Printed in the United States
By Bookmasters